AmericanGirl Library®

room for you

Find Your Style and Make Your Room Say You!

illustrated by
Shawn Banner

AmericanGirl®

Published by Pleasant Company Publications

Visit our Web site at **americangirl.com**

Printed in the United States of America.

04 05 06 07 08 09 WCR 12 11 10 9 8 7 6 5

American Girl Library® is a registered trademark of American Girl, LLC.

Editorial Development: Julie Williams, Michelle Watkins

Contributors: Mary D'Alton, Sarah Jane Brian, Cheryl Cox, Sherri Haab

Art Direction & Design: Chris Lorette David

Production: Kendra Pulvermacher, Janette Sowinski

Library of Congress Cataloging-in-Publication Data

Room for you : make your room say you! : find your style / illustrated by Shawn Banner.

p. cm. "American girl library"

ISBN 1-58485-369-7

1. Handicraft—Juvenile literature. 2. Girls' bedrooms—Juvenile literature. 3. Interior decoration—Juvenile literature. [1. Interior decoration. 2. Bedrooms. 3. Handicraft.] I. Banner, Shawn, ill. II. American girl (Middleton, Wis.)

TT171 .R66 2001

747.7′7—dc21   2001022880

Contents

Too Messy?   Too Blah?

Too Crowded?   Too Small?

Too Baby?   Make It Say You!

Your Room

You hang out there. You tell secrets there. You sleep there. You dream there. **It's your room.** What better place to be yourself than in your room?

When you walk into your room, you should feel **comfy, happy,** and even a little **psyched** because you're surrounded by things that you love. But do you feel that way? Can you be yourself in your own space? Take a hard look at your room. **Really look at it.** Have your hair thingies taken over your dresser? When was the last time you sat in that chair? Is your bed-spread way out of date?

As you've gotten older, chances are your **likes and dislikes have changed** while your **room has stayed the same.** Or maybe you've just gotten used to the way things are. Whatever the case, it's time to **make your room say you.** Take the first step and quiz yourself to **reveal your style.** Then get great decorating ideas to help you **express your person-ality** and create a room that reflects **who you are today.**

And don't forget to check in with the **Room Doctor** for **advice** on how to share a room, keep private things private, and make cleaning fun—well, at least bearable. And if you think your room is **too messy, too small, too baby,** or **too blah,** you're not alone. Turn to the **Girls' Fix-It Guide** for terrific tips on making your room **just right for you.**

Interior Design 101

Keep these **basic decorating ideas** in mind when you re-do your room.

Keep one piece of furniture as the focus of the room. Make it something you really love! When you walk into the room, your eye should naturally fall on one object that makes you feel right at home. If one thing doesn't rule the room, you may have to tackle some clutter.

You don't have to spend a lot of money. "Shop" the house—attic, basement, or garage—for objects that you can re-do and move into your room. Garage sales, flea markets, and secondhand stores are also full of cheap, used furniture and decorative stuff that you can fix up to look just like new. Just keep your eyes open and your imagination bubbling.

You don't have to spend ANY money at all! Out of dough? Make a quick and easy change to your room simply by moving stuff around and putting things in new places. Drag your dresser to a new spot. Frame a favorite photo of your pooch. Push your bed up against a different wall. Just waking up on the other side of the room can seem like a fresh start!

Be creative! Think about how you can turn the ordinary into the extraordinary. Glue fringe around a lampshade. Sprinkle glitter in your dresser drawers and cover it with clear contact paper. A trip to the craft or fabric store will give you lots of great ideas.

Don't be in a hurry to fill your room with stuff. Leave space for that perfect chair or table that is sure to come along later. You'll know it when you see it!

Plan it out. If you'd like to make a big change—like rearranging furniture or hanging things from the ceiling—sketch out your dream room and give your parents a preview. You'll need their O.K.—especially when making permanent changes like painting walls—and maybe their help, too!

Quiz!
What's Your Style?

Circle the answer that describes you best.

1. When you blow out the candles on your 16th birthday, **you'll wish for . . .**

a. a limousine with a sunroof so you can wave to your "fans."

b. an SUV to explore roads less traveled.

c. a cute Beetle bug to give your friends a lift in.

d. a racy red sports car to dart about town in.

2. Which **painting** would stop you in your tracks at the museum?

a.

b.

c.

d.
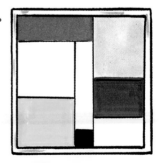

3. Which **color** do you like best?

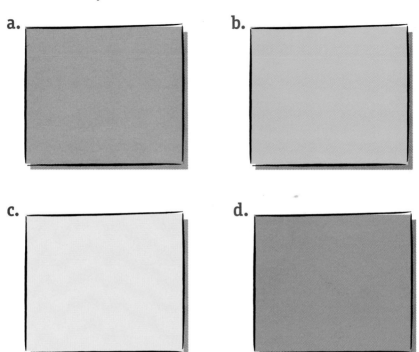

a.

b.

c.

d.

4. Hurray, **it's Saturday!** You plan to . . .

a. learn all the words to your favorite new song.

b. go to the park.

c. phone friends and write to pen pals.

d. surf the Net.

5. Your **favorite wild animal** is a . . .

a. leopard.

b. dolphin.

c. koala.

d. polar bear.

6. You've just been elected President of the United States! The **first thing** you plan to do is . . .

a. invite your favorite artists or musicians to perform at the White House.

b. find homes for the homeless.

c. travel around the country visiting small towns.

d. make the cities safer places to live.

7. Which **poster** would you hang in your room?

a. a movie poster

b. a rainforest poster

c. a butterfly poster

d. a "Go For It!" poster

8. Surprise! Mom lets you keep the stray kitten you found. **You name your new pet . . .**

a. Disco.

b. Tiger.

c. Snowball.

d. Simon.

9. You're most likely to **dot your i's** with . . .

a. stars.

b. flowers.

c. tiny hearts.

d. little circles.

10. When you invite a new friend over, the **first thing** you show her is . . .

a. your autograph book.

b. your seashell collection.

c. your scrapbook.

d. your scooter.

11. Roses are red, violets are blue, **which bouquet** would you choose?

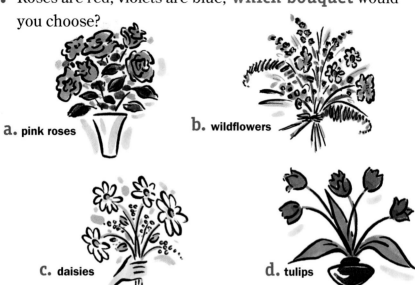

a. pink roses

b. wildflowers

c. daisies

d. tulips

12. Your **favorite subject** at school is . . .

a. English. You love to write stories and poems.

b. Science. You love to study nature and find out how things work.

c. Social studies. You love learning about different people, places, and things.

d. Math. You love geometric shapes and figuring out the answers.

13. Which **hair thingie** would you most likely wear?

a. lots of little rhinestone bobby pins

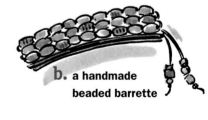

b. a handmade beaded barrette

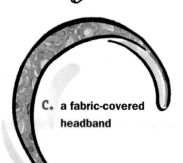

c. a fabric-covered headband

d. a sleek silver barrette

14. The one thing in your bedroom that **you couldn't live without** is . . .

a. a phone.

b. a window.

c. a mirror.

d. your computer.

15. A **dream summer vacation** would be to . . .

a. go on tour with your favorite band.

b. dig for dinosaur fossils in Montana.

c. visit your pen pal in England.

d. spend a week in a big city.

16. You're **decorating** a plain white picture frame. Which items would you glue to it?

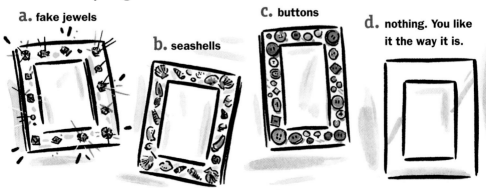

a. fake jewels

b. seashells

c. buttons

d. nothing. You like it the way it is.

17. Your **favorite pj's** are . . .

a. a silky pajama top and bottoms set.

b. an oversize T-shirt.

c. a floral-print nightgown.

d. matching blue flannel top and bottoms with white clouds.

18. Pick a **purse!**

a. a purple sequined handbag

b. a fanny pack

c. a pink shoulder bag with daisy appliques

d. a black messenger bag that leaves your hands free

19. Which **comforter** would you cover your bed with?

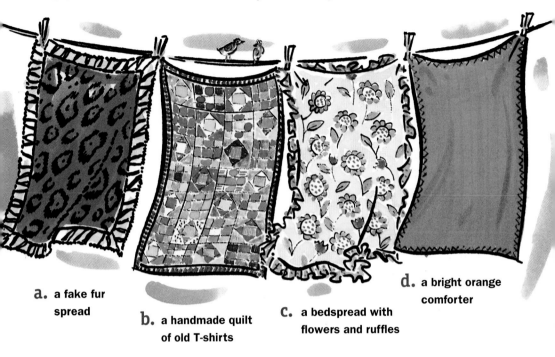

a. a fake fur spread

b. a handmade quilt of old T-shirts

c. a bedspread with flowers and ruffles

d. a bright orange comforter

20. At the **amusement park**, you can be found waiting in line for . . .

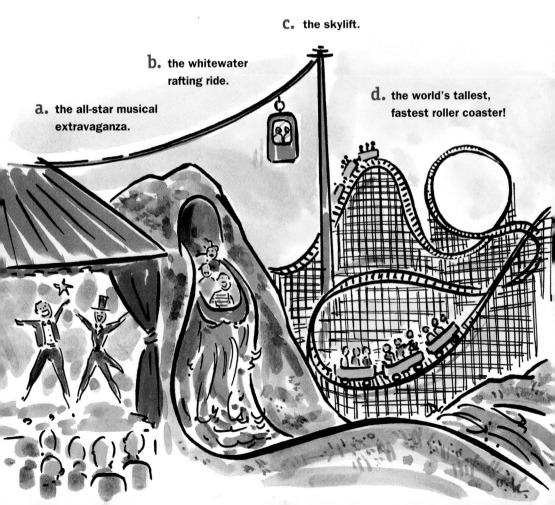

a. the all-star musical extravaganza.

b. the whitewater rafting ride.

c. the skylift.

d. the world's tallest, fastest roller coaster!

21. The **first charm** you'd put on your new charm bracelet would be . . .

a. a moon and star.

b. a peace symbol.

c. a silver heart engraved with your initials.

d. a yin-yang symbol.

22. What was your **favorite book** when you were little?

a. *Eloise* by Kay Thompson

b. *Where the Wild Things Are* by Maurice Sendak

c. *The Complete Tales of Winnie-the-Pooh* by A.A. Milne

d. *The Cat in the Hat* by Dr. Seuss

23. You're going to **write a friend** a note. Which stationery do you choose?

a. purple paper with silver stars

b. recycled paper

c. a notecard with a border of hearts

d. none. You send an e-mail instead.

Now find your style!

Count how many of each letter you circled to find out!

a's ___ **b's** ___ **c's** ___ **d's** ___

Mostly **a's**

You're a *Sparkly Girl!*

Turn to **page 18** and get glamorous.

Mostly **b's**

You're a *Nature Girl!*

Turn to **page 30** and go wild.

Mostly **C's**

You're a *Sunny Girl!*

Turn to **page 42** and start shining.

Mostly **d's**

You're a *Bold Girl!*

Turn to **page 54** and get graphic.

Mix It Up

You don't have to stick to just one style! Look through each section for lots of quick and easy decorating ideas. The most important thing is that you **love your room** when you're finished!

Sparkly Girl

Your style is **glamorous and dramatic.** Your starry eyes are caught by all that **glitters.** You love **rich, bright colors** in shades of purple, pink, and blue. Soft and luxurious fabrics like **fake fur** and **tutu tulle** fit your style. And when it comes to the latest trends, **you know what's hot** and what's not. Your imagination soars sky-high, and you're attracted to the moon and the stars—which **shine just like you!**

movie stars

e-mail

sunglasses

parties

fashion mags

anything that sparkles!

night sky

music

Glam Lounge

You want a room with a touch of drama—where dreamy things can happen and where you can pamper yourself silly. So bring on the sparkle and transform your space into a glamorous lounge fit for a star!

Start by turning your bed into a glamorous couch. Simply push a twin bed against a wall, cover it with a satiny comforter, and line the wall with lots of fringed and furry pillows to lean on. If you have a trundle bed and are expecting friends, pull the bottom bed out a bit to create a "stair step" for additional seating. Your audience is ready to be entertained!

Decorate your lounge with all that glitters— sequins, rhinestones, mirrors, seed beads—whatever! If it catches the light, it's right for your room. Cover accessories like frames and notebooks with glistening seed beads. Glue or tape mini mirrors (available at craft stores) in pretty patterns on a wall. Add sequin trim to pillowcases and curtains.

Perk up the floor of your lounge with a shaggy rug in white or purple. Drape a sturdy cardboard box with shiny metallic fabric for a cheap but chic coffee table or nightstand. Top it with glitter picture frame domes, an autograph book, and a stack of movie star mags.

Make your space twinkle with tiny lights. Wrap a string or two of clear holiday lights around your window, shelves, or bedposts. Or drape them around your primping mirror and set them to blink for some real Hollywood style.

Now add star power. Hang movie posters using silver and gold star stickers instead of tape. Frame an enlarged copy of your favorite star's autograph (check the fan mags)—or just use your own. After all, you're the star in your room! Cut celestial shapes out of metallic craft paper and attach them to the ceiling above your bed, where they'll catch the light and your eye. And when it's time to tuck in, you can kick off your fluffy slippers and . . . wish upon a star.

Starstruck

☆ **silver sign**

Add some sparkle to your name. Trace the letters of your name onto a thick piece of cardboard, making them about 6 inches tall. Cut them out and wrap with foil, scrunching it up as you go. Hang them on a wall or bulletin board, or prop them up on a small ledge or shelf.

☆ **lights, camera, action!**

Turn your room into a movie set with a director's chair. Add your name on the back with glittery fabric paint. Keep an extra one folded in the closet for superstar friends to pull out when they visit.

☆ head shots

Staple black-and-white photo-booth picture strips onto a wide strip of zebra-striped ribbon. Tie a bow at the top of the strip, and tack it to your wall. (You can also stick i-Zone Polaroids onto the ribbon.)

☆ shine on, superstar

Glue sparkly strips of sequin trim around the edges of a clear plastic poster frame. Add a picture of your favorite movie star!

☆ curtain call

Use a glitter-glue pen to add dazzling dots to a pair of sheer white curtains. Accent the glitter with holographic or Mylar ribbon tie-backs.

☆ makeup, please

Hang a frosted plastic shower bucket with suction cups under your mirror. Use it to store hair thingies and other primping supplies.

☆ feather your nest!

Glue a marabou feather boa around the top of a frosted plastic waste-paper basket, and drape another one around your mirror, *dah-ling*.

☆ it's a wrap

Place a clean glass jar in the center of a square of sparkly fabric. Gather up the edges of the fabric around the jar, and slip a couple of shiny hair elastics around the neck to hold the fabric in place. Store autograph pens inside.

☆ star tracks

Draw or trace a star shape (as large as possible) on the back of a rubber-backed plush bath mat. Cover your workspace (you'll create a bit of a mess!), and ask an adult to help you cut out the shape. Make several rugs in different colors and arrange a star-studded path to your bed!

Pop Princess

☆ wispy windows

Soften your windows with a flowing fabric swag. Attach three stick-on hooks to the wall above your window—one on the far left, one in the center, and one on the far right. Drape a long piece of chiffon over the hooks, gathering the fabric at each hook and tying on a small silver ribbon to hold it in place.

☆ kiss me!

With adhesive Velcro, attach a plastic photo sleeve to the tummy of a well-loved stuffed animal. Slip a picture of your prince charming or fairy godmother into the sleeve.

☆ candle in the window

Starting at the top, wrap a battery-operated candlestick with self-adhesive glitter dot tape or blue-star holographic tape. Finish it off by gluing a piece of marabou around the base. Place it in your window and light up the night!

☆ mirror, mirror

Glue metallic pom-poms around the frame of a large hand mirror. Now who's the fairest one of all?

☆ breakfast in bed

Sprinkle the top of a white "breakfast-in-bed" tray with glitter and spangles, then cover with clear contact paper. Perfect for holding study snacks or writing fan letters in bed!

☆ pretty pedestals

Gather a few empty cans or small boxes of different heights. Arrange them on a wall shelf or on top of a bookcase with the taller objects toward the back. Drape a large piece of satin over the objects. Display trophies, collectibles, dolls, or anything you think deserves to be put on a pedestal!

☆ dreamy drape

You'll feel like a princess under this canopy. Separate an embroidery hoop and tie 4 pieces of ribbon onto the larger hoop. Gather the other ends above and tie them in a knot. Center the smaller hoop underneath the middle of a long piece of tulle. Press the larger hoop on top, sandwiching the fabric and ribbon. Tighten the hoop. Ask an adult to help you hang the canopy above your bed using a screw hook. Tie the ends of the fabric to your bedposts or headboard for extra drama!

Bedazzle

☆ disco decor
Make your own disco ball! Screw a small hook into the top of a Styrofoam ball. Glue on mini mirrors (available at craft stores). When dry, hang from your ceiling, shine a spotlight on it, and start dancing.

☆ desk dazzlers
Dress up your desk accessories with sparkly seed beads. Cover the flat surface of a stapler, pen, box, or pencil holder with heavy-duty, double-stick mounting tape. Roll the taped surface in sparkly micro-beads and bugle beads until covered.

☆ time flies

Glue colored feathers around the frame of a plain clock. Glue each feather at an angle, overlapping as you glue the next one on. Let dry. Then watch time fly!

☆ sun sparklers
Tie a piece of fishing line around an old CD. Decorate with glittery fabric paint and a few rhinestones. Hang in your window and watch it sparkle in the sunlight.

☆ cozy keyboard pillow
Pamper your wrists while e-mailing or instant messaging. Sprinkle the back side of a 20-inch square piece of velvet with dried lavender. Roll up, folding over 2 inches of the fabric at a time. Tie the ends off with holographic twisty ties or ribbon.

☆ pulls with pizzazz
Add instant glamour to your dresser drawers. Paint plain wood drawer pulls with acrylic paint. Let dry. Glue on rhinestones or jewels and let dry again. Then ask an adult to help you screw the pulls onto your dresser drawers.

☆ photo bouquet

Fill a glass vase with purple marbles. Cut 2 or 3 different lengths of 18-gauge wire (available at hardware stores). Twist one end of each wire into a flat curl. Stick the straight end into the glass and tuck a photo into the curl.

☆ **gem image**
Glue fake jewels around the frame of a full-length dressing mirror.

☆ **dripping with jewels**
Drape silver beaded garland or shiny Mardi Gras beads around your room to create a bejeweled look.

Plush Pad

tie-dyed wall
Use thumbtacks to hang a richly colored tie-dyed sheet on the wall behind your bed or desk for a splashy backdrop.

fringe benefit
Glue silver or beaded fringe along the edges of a wall shelf, on a lamp shade, or onto the edge of furniture.

plush headboard
Drape a large piece of plush fabric over your headboard so that it hangs evenly in front and in back of the board and the ends stick out a little on each side. Use self-adhesive Velcro strips to hold the sides together.

psychedelic pillow
Dress up an old pillow with a psychedelic scarf. Lay a square pillow diagonally on top of a square scarf. Knot the opposite corners of the scarf around the pillow.

groovy curtain

Hang a colored beaded curtain in front of your window.

fuzzy closet

Line the inside of your closet door with a large piece of pink plush using tacks or self-adhesive Velcro. You'll feel warm 'n fuzzy every time you look inside!

fur your eyes only

Warm up your computer monitor with fake fur trim. Cut strips of plush fabric to size and attach around the monitor with self-adhesive Velcro.

Nature Girl

You're wild about the **Earth** and dream of surrounding yourself with **animals, plants, flowers,** and **wide-open spaces.** You would gladly trade your bedroom for a greenhouse, tree house, cabin, or houseboat. Scenic views, fresh air, hiking trails, bright sunlight, and cuddly critters bring out the **call of the wild** in you.

dragonflies

sunrise

ocean

wild animals

seashells

exploring

sailboats

birds

Freshen Up

Let your imagination run wild and make what's old new again. Hunt for **hidden treasures,** like wooden chairs or old picture frames, at flea markets, garage sales, and thrift stores. Give them a new paint job, decorate with a stencil or two, and they'll be good as new.

Even your own garage or basement may hold a Cinderella story or two. Bring a plastic **lawn chair** in from the cold. Clean it up and soften it with a seat cushion for an easy and inexpensive place to relax.

It's important for you to **keep nature in sight.** And the best view of all is through your bedroom window. Brighten up gray winter days by painting **bright white snowflakes** on your window panes with tempera paint. When spring has sprung, hang a **clear crystal** in front of the window and watch rays of colored light bounce off the walls as it catches the sunlight. It's **your very own rainbow!**

Cover your walls with pictures of breathtaking views. Put together a **jigsaw puzzle** of a lush landscape. When finished, glue it together and frame it. Collect **postcards of natural wonders** and use them to make a border around the top of the walls in your room.

Or buy a disposable **panoramic camera** and capture scenic views or pretty sunsets on your next vacation. Display your photos in panoramic frames to remind you of your trip.

Freshen up your room by bringing the outdoors indoors. Wash out **pretty drink bottles** and use them to hold **fresh clippings** from the garden. Use **big stones** as bookends—available in your own back-yard or at garden stores. Glue **twigs** to an old head-board or to a picture frame. You can even lay down a **fake grass doormat** beside your bed. When you rise and shine, you can make believe that's real **grass tickling your toes!**

Secret Retreat

 puppy pillow
Want to sleep with your puppy every night? Find a cute picture of your pet and enlarge it on a color copier—11-by-17 inches should be large enough for a standard-size pillowcase. Next, copy the enlargement directly onto iron-on transfer paper (available at office supply stores and copy centers). Then ask an adult to help you iron the picture onto your pillowcase.

 nature's call
Play a nature CD of birds singing, crickets chirping, or a rainstorm (available at nature stores). Or record your own the next time you go for a hike.

it's alive!

Make color copies of a favorite poster and cut out details—butterflies, birds, whatever—from the copies. Trace cut-outs onto a thin piece of cardboard or foam, cut them out, and glue together. Using double-stick tape or poster putty, place the cut-outs on the wall to look as if they're "flying" off the poster. You can even use straight pins to put a couple on your curtains.

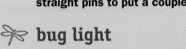

bug light

Glue lifelike fabric butterflies onto a lamp shade, and you'll feel as if you never left camp!

kitty treat

Plant cat grass (also known as wheat or oat grass) in a pot to keep your kitty happy and to remind you both of the great outdoors!

branch out

Measure the width of your window and find a branch about the same size from your yard. Sand down any rough edges and make sure it's bug-free and clean. Put tab-top curtains on the branch and hang it on brackets.

you rock!

Create a message written in stone. Knead and shape a piece of Sculpey Granitex clay into a stone shape. Use a toothpick to write a message like "Peace" or "You rock!" into the clay. Ask an adult to help you bake it as directed on the clay's packaging. When cool, dab paint into the carved letters and let dry.

a library branch . . .

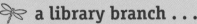

of your very own! Find 2 branches about one foot long and one inch thick. Tie one end of each branch onto one piece of rope and the other end onto another piece of rope, spacing them apart to create a ladder effect. Tie the 2 ropes together at the top. Then hang on a wall and drape magazines over the branches.

Explorer's Lounge

✥ safari sounds
Set the mood with a CD of wild animal sounds and other natural noises—elephants trumpeting, birds cawing, thunder crashing.

✥ it's a zoo in there
For a wild surprise, line your dresser drawers with zebra-striped or other animal-print wrapping paper.

✥ globe-trotter gadgets
Keep a globe on your desk to plan your next trip. Wrap gift boxes with old maps and use them to store photos and travel brochures. Hang a compass nearby so you'll always know which direction is home.

✥ adventure of a lifetime
Cover a corkboard with a map of where you'd love to go, then decorate it with postcards and other things that remind you of your dream trip.

✥ a new leaf
Display pretty leaves from the backyard or from a flower arrangement in clip frames.

✥ light the way
Line a clear plastic Paper-It light-switch plate with a map of your favorite continent.

✥ spotted seat
Traveling girls need their rest! Wrap the back of an old wooden chair in fake fur for a cozy perch. Fold a piece of spotted plush over the back, then trim fabric to cover the length of the seat back. Hold the sides of the plush together and fold them back, wrapping one over the other. Secure with a long strip of self-adhesive Velcro.

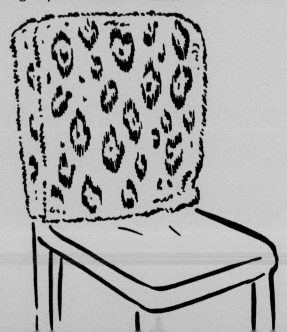

grow your own jungle

Arrange a variety of plants in colored
pots on an old TV tray. Pour small
pebbles and rocks onto the tray
around the pots. Place a lifelike
plastic frog or lizard in the tray for a
jungle surprise.

Recycled Treasures

❧ T-shirt pillow

Dress up a tired throw pillow with a favorite T-shirt. Put the pillow inside the tee. Pull the shirt tightly around the pillow, making sure any picture or slogan is centered on the front of the pillow. Then tie a knot in each sleeve and on both sides of the bottom hem.

clipboard frame

Find an old clipboard and decorate it with stickers or paint the back-board a new color. Hang it on a wall and clip on a picture or an important note. It's easy to change what you have framed!

task baskets

Use last year's Easter baskets to hold letters, cards, or important school papers. Use one for "hot" things that you need to take care of right away and another for "cool" things, like catalogues, that you just can't bear to throw away.

cut the grass

Bring your boring cork bulletin board back to life. Glue or staple a piece of Astroturf over the cork.

pencil pot

Find a pretty teapot that's no longer used for brewing tea, and put pencils in it. A matching teacup and saucer would look great sitting nearby filled with paper clips and erasers.

calendar cut-outs

Hate to toss out old calendars with all those pretty pictures? Recycle them! Cut out a cute picture. Place the cut-out on top of a thick sheet of fun foam and trace around it. Cut out the shape that you traced on the foam. Now glue the picture onto the front. Make a stand by cutting a triangle out of the foam sheet and taping it onto the back at a right angle.

game table

Glue an old board game like Life or Monopoly to the top of an old TV tray, milk crate, or plastic outdoor table.

Just Beachy

made in the shade

Set a colorful beach or patio umbrella near your bed for a cool canopy. Place it in an umbrella stand or a large bucket of sand.

aloha

Drape flower leis over your bed-posts, chairs, or dressing mirror.

sea souvenirs

Place a bamboo placemat on top of your nightstand. Top with a jar of sand art or a shell filled with sea glass.

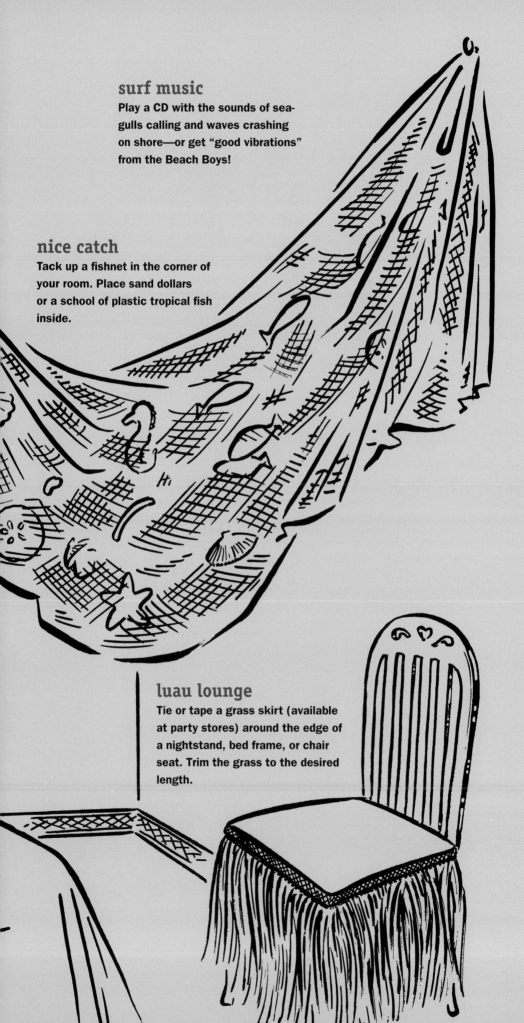

surf music

Play a CD with the sounds of sea-
gulls calling and waves crashing
on shore—or get "good vibrations"
from the Beach Boys!

nice catch

Tack up a fishnet in the corner of
your room. Place sand dollars
or a school of plastic tropical fish
inside.

luau lounge

Tie or tape a grass skirt (available
at party stores) around the edge of
a nightstand, bed frame, or chair
seat. Trim the grass to the desired
length.

Sunny Girl

Bright, warm colors and **pretty patterns** fit your friendly, cheerful style. You like colors that glow because they're sure to bring a smile. Little extras like **soft ruffles** and **fabric flowers** sweeten the feel of your room. And all those **pictures of family** and **friends** grinning back at you prove that you're **all heart.**

butterflies

crafts

secret notes

daisies

scrapbooks

MEMORY BOOK

hearts

comfy sneakers

Social Butterfly

You're quick to smile and make friends laugh. You love to chat and giggle about everything under the sun. So it's no wonder that you'll soar in a room that's as bright and cheerful as you.

Wake up your walls with luscious lime or fuzzy peach paint. The bright colors are sure to match your style. Dress your bed with a cotton candy-colored comforter and plenty of plump pillows. Add a sweet-smelling sachet to the pile of cushions, and you'll get a whiff of fragrance every time you climb into bed. Place your diary on your nightstand so you can write about your dreams and thoughts at a moment's notice.

Don't forget how special the little touches can be. Look around your room. There are probably a lot of things you can use to decorate. Plant your pens and pencils in a pretty vase. Drape a straw hat on your bedpost. Fill a glass jar with conversation hearts. Place a couple of tiny tart tins on your dresser to hold scrunchies and ponytail ties. Cluster your collection of figurines on top of your dresser. Frame a favorite poem or quote and hang it by the door. It'll be plain for friends to see what makes you happy!

Keep a steamer trunk at the foot of your bed. Fill it with old quilts and blankets. When you feel the urge to hang out, spread the quilts and blankets on the

floor and top with pillows for a perfect place to read, talk on the phone, cuddle with your pup, or just giggle with friends. And since a social butterfly like you is bound to have lots of friends visit, create a scrapbook of smiles to remember them by. Take a picture of each visitor who comes through your bedroom door, and keep the photos in a book along with the date and a note about what you did together.

Girl Gallery

✿ rickrack picture

Glue rickrack around the edge of a plain wooden picture frame. Tape or tack a bowed ribbon onto the back of the frame to hang it.

✿ bear chair

Hang a doll-size chair on a wall and sit your favorite teddy bear on it. He'll love hanging out there!

✿ poster pins

Here's a cute way to hang artwork—without punching holes in the corners or going to the trouble of framing. Use a highlighter to add some color to two large spring-clamp clothespins. Let dry. Put a small piece of heavy-duty double-stick mounting tape on the back of each clothespin, and press the pins on the wall where you'd like your artwork to hang. Now just clip up your masterpiece.

hanging scrapbook

Got a stack of photos, ticket stubs, birthday cards, or doodles from friends that you're not quite ready to hide away in your scrapbook? Hang a piece of silk cord across a wall and clip on photos, postcards, and other mementos with mini clothespins.

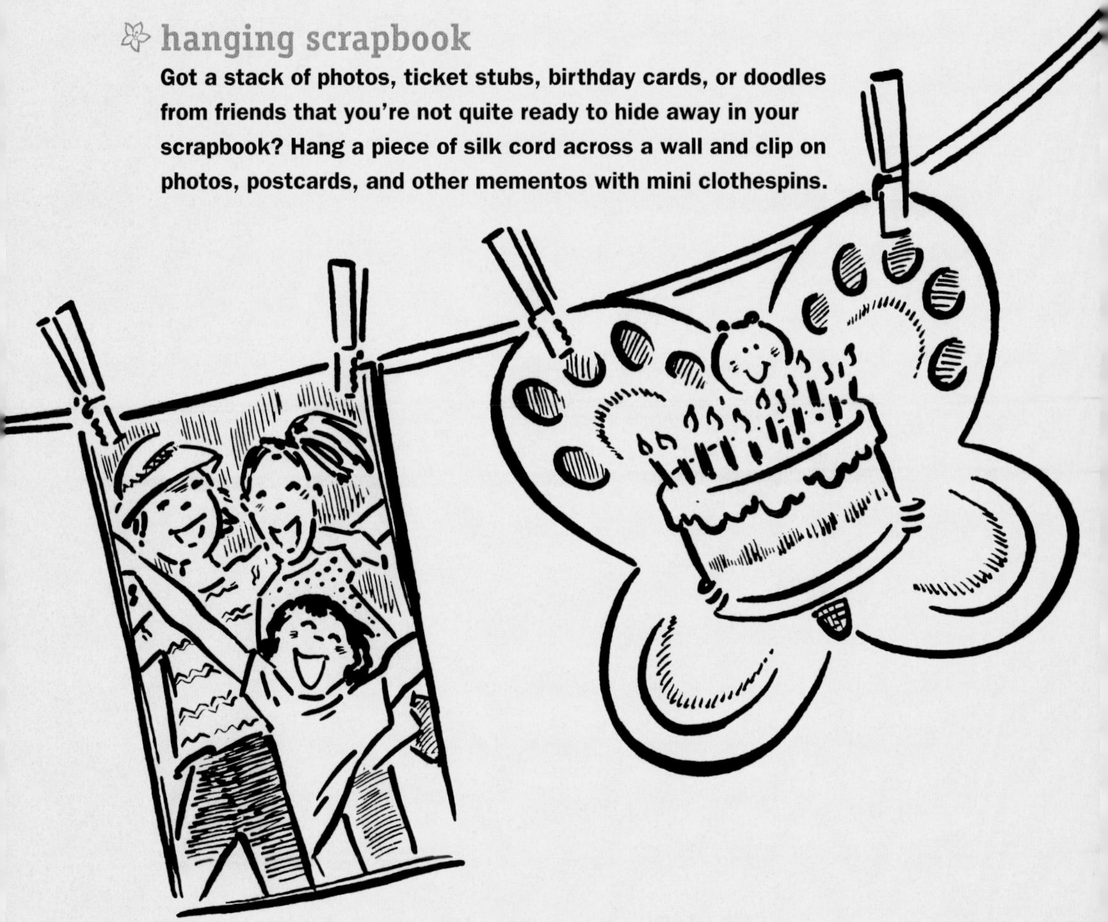

switch-plate greetings

Recycle favorite greeting cards into switch-plate art. Cut the back off a greeting card. Measure and cut a hole for the switch in the middle of the card. Attach the card to the top of the plate with removable tape or poster putty. Change the greeting with the season!

picture pattern

Hang photos in eye-pleasing patterns and groupings. Voila! Your very own photo gallery. Hint: hang the largest frame in the center and smaller ones to the sides.

Sweet Suite

✿ twilight

Put a pink lightbulb in a decorative lamp to create a soothing glow. For a special touch, drape a pretty jeweled metal chain over the top of the shade.

✤ butterfly tiebacks

Use butterfly hair clips to hold your curtains back from the window and let the sun shine in!

✤ grooming rack

Decorate and hang a kitchen spice rack above your dresser or desk. Fill it with grooming goodies like your brush, hair clips, lip gloss, and a mirror.

✤ secret note pouch

Tie a small canvas bag to the back of your desk chair and tuck notes from friends into it.

✤ sweet storage

Use empty candy boxes or mint tins to hold little things like paper clips, buttons, coins, or stamps. Cover the containers with stickers, leftover wrapping paper, or pretty contact paper.

✤ kitty mobile

Tie cat toys onto an embroidery hoop and dangle it from a plant hanger about waist-high from the floor. Keep a soft pillow or padded stool underneath, and your kitty may never want to leave your room!

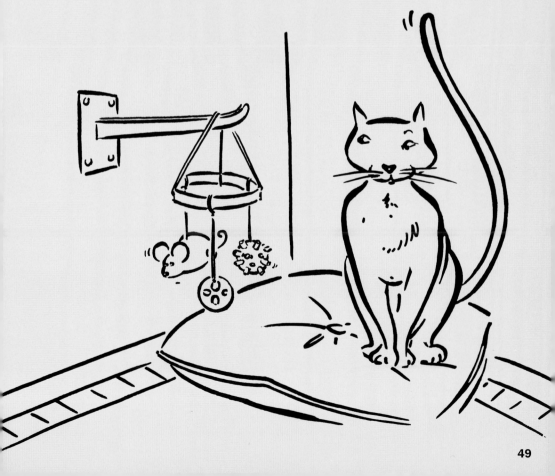

Touch of Charm

❀ window braid

Hang 3 different-colored sheer curtain panels on a rod. Loosely braid them together. Tie off your braid with a piece of bright ribbon or a pretty napkin ring.

❀ bedside basket

Ask an adult to help you hang an old bicycle basket on the wall near your bed. Store books and magazines inside.

❀ twinkle, twinkle

Use a safety pin to punch tiny holes into a plain white lamp shade. Turn the lamp on, and you'll see pretty dots of light twinkling through the pinholes.

❀ initial it

Buy large wooden letters in your initials or to spell a favorite word. Paint the letters a bright color and let dry. Decorate with stickers, or decoupage words and pics clipped from magazines. Hang the letters on your bedroom door to give visitors clues to you!

❀ skirt shade

Add charm to a plain lamp with a ruffly child's or doll's skirt. First find a frilly skirt and a shade to fit. Then stretch or glue the waistband of the skirt around the top of the shade.

❀ dressy doorknob

Hang colorful sparkly bracelets around your doorknob for a warm welcome.

❀ hat rack

Hang a folding coat rack in your room and use it to display fancy hats, pretty purses, and silky scarves. You can even use the purses to store jewelry and other little items that tend to clutter up your dresser.

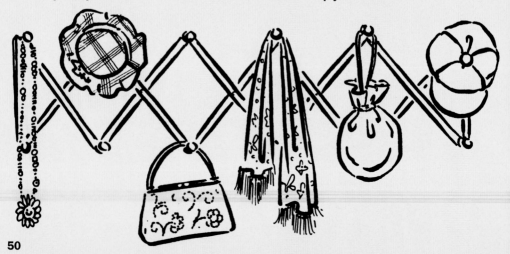

✿ charming chair

Drape a piece of tulle or other light, sheer material around the back of a chair. Gather the fabric in the back and tie a fabric flower or small bow around it.

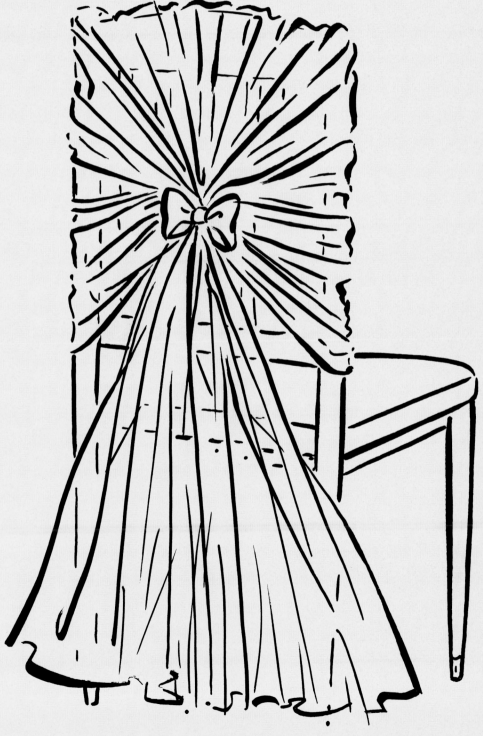

Room to Bloom

tweet, tweet
Put an ivy plant in a bird cage and hang it from your ceiling.

garden headboard
Create a headboard that'll keep your dreams blooming. Ask an adult to help you make it. Buy a small picket fence kit at a local garden or hardware store. Measure the width of your bed and assemble a section of picket fence to fit. Slide the fencing behind the head of your bed, and push the bed up against it to hold it in place.

nice 'n easy nightstand
Turn an ordinary wooden stool into a dreamy nightstand. Top with a pretty scarf or cloth napkin and your diary. Add a bright lamp to light up the page while you write about your day.

flowerfall

Create a cascade of flowers in your window. Use tiny safety pins to attach fabric flowers to a pair of sheer curtains.

everlasting blooms

Make fluffy flowers out of tissue paper and pipe cleaners. Plant them in a pretty vase filled with marbles. No water needed!

petal pulls

Dress up your drawers. Paint the top of round drawer pulls bright yellow and let dry. Cut flower shapes out of a sheet of fun foam and snip an X in the middle of each. Slip the flower shapes over the drawer pulls.

Bold Girl

You're cool in a room with **smooth, sleek surfaces** and **little clutter.** Keeping things neat helps you stay focused on your goals, but your playful side often wins out! You're always on the move, so it's no surprise that you like **bright, bold colors** and **graphic patterns** with **geometric shapes** to go along with all that energy!

quiz shows

surfing the Internet

extreme sports

comics and cartoons

polka dots

games

Colorburst

Bold colors and stripes are attention-getters—just like you! Your space needs lots of **playful patterns** to reflect your get-up-and-go style. **Be creative!** Paint a large **turquoise** square on the wall near the top of your bed for a faux headboard. Or paint one wall in **outrageous orange** and the others in **bright white.** Dot the walls with colored round stickers. For an eye-opening surprise, paint the inside of your closet **bright yellow.** You'll get a charge every morning when you look inside.

Your bed will make a strong statement when covered with "mismatched" linens. Mix **striped sheets** with **polka-dot pillowcases,** then top with a solid color comforter to tie it all together. Don't forget to add a **bed skirt** to give your bed a clean, complete look.

Brighten up your computer corner by painting each desk drawer a **different color.** Replace boring drawer pulls with **frosted plastic** or **shiny silver** ones in fun geometric shapes. Keep things moving in a comfy desk chair with **wheels.**

Think big about what to put on your walls. **One large poster** or graphic image may be more suited to your style than lots of little pictures everywhere. Hang **old vinyl records** or used **CDs** on the wall for an instant

graphic effect. Or bring out the inner artist in you—**splatter paint** onto a prestretched canvas and display it for all to see.

Give a ho-hum corner a funky feel with a **curvy, comfy butterfly chair.** You can change the cover from one color to another when you need a new look. Recycle a **metal filing cabinet** into a nightstand or side table and fill it with CDs. Accessorize with lots of **frosted plastic stuff** like a clock and wastebasket. And to finish off your funky corner, add a **lava lamp.** The flowing liquid lumps will calm you at the end of your **busy, bold-girl day.**

Get Graphic

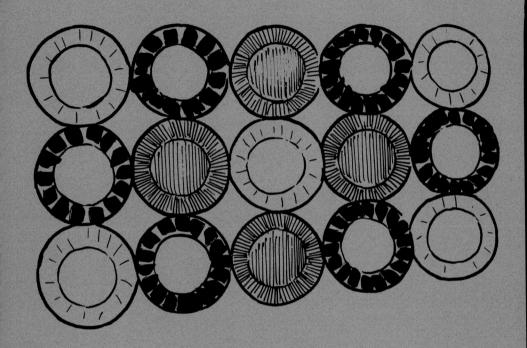

☀ 3-D walls

Cover a wall with colored plastic or paper plates for a cool 3-D effect. Put double-stick tape on the back of the plates and, starting at the very top of the wall, stick them in nice, neat rows. Cover one wall from top to bottom. Once you get the hang of it, you can make fun patterns and shapes by using contrasting colored plates.

☀ checkerboard rug

Make your own rug using square carpet samples. Buy different colored pieces on sale at home decorating or carpet stores. Turn the squares over, arrange them into a pattern, and tape them together with packing or electrical tape.

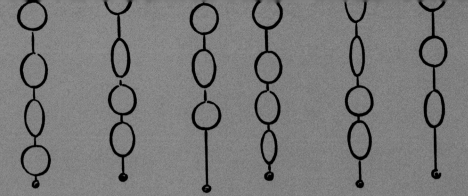

✴ dotted line

Make dots float in the air! Press colored round stickers back-to-back onto long pieces of filament or fishing line. Tie a bead at the end of each line to weigh it down. Then tie the dotted lines onto a curtain rod and hang them in front of a window or over your door.

✴ room reflex

Reflect the light with safety stripes. Add strips of reflective tape to curtains, rugs, or furniture.

✴ stripe light

Perk up a plain white lamp shade with bright ribbon. Using fabric glue, attach satin ribbons of different widths and colors around a barrel shade—one with sides that are straight, not slanted or sloping.

✴ shooting stars

Put strips of masking tape on a wall to form fun shapes—asterisks, squares, or diamonds. Paint over them and let dry. Remove tape to reveal a great graphic pattern.

✴ on target

Use a drawing compass to draw a few circles onto a piece of felt, making them smaller and smaller as you go. Cut the circles out and glue them on top of each other to make a target. Then glue the targets onto a polar fleece blanket or a plain pillow.

✴ typographic

Graffiti your walls with letters, numbers, and punctuation marks. Place a sheet of transfer type against the wall and rub the back of the letters with a pencil. You can spell words or messages—or just let the letters float wherever you like.

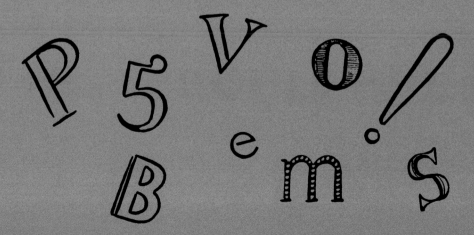

Fantastic Plastic

☀ see-through pillow

Using double-stick tape, tape two square pieces of clear vinyl together on three sides. Stuff with colored pom-poms, Styrofoam peanuts, or shredded paper. Tape the last side closed, blowing air into the pillow just before you seal it up.

☀ plastic pockets

Hang a row of plastic pockets by your desk, and store school or art supplies, trading cards, and other favorite things.

☀ wavy display

Cut the sides off a wide egg carton and paint it a cool color with acrylic paint. When dry, toss loose change, candy, or jewelry into the little cups—or display an arrangement of apples and bananas on top.

☀ roller coasters

Cut a wavy shape out of a sheet of fun foam and use it as a mouse pad. Make smaller shapes to use as drink coasters.

☀ cool curtains

Shower curtains come in bright colors and eye-popping plastic patterns. So why not use one as a window curtain? Cut a shower curtain to fit your window and hang it from a curtain rod using small ball chains or empty key rings.

☀ pez perch

Got a wide molding above your window or door? Use it to display your Pez dispenser collection or other small collectibles.

☀ rubber-band board
Stretch brightly colored rubber bands tightly across a cork bulletin board, securing the bands at each end of the board with pushpins. Place several in a row to make stripes. Or add vertical bands to create squares. Slip photos or cards behind the bands to display.

☀ dice box
Round up a bunch of old dice all the same size, or buy dice at a gaming or hobby store. Glue them together to make a keepsake box or use them to decorate picture frames, shelving, or anything that needs a touch of whimsy!

Play Room

☀ slinky frame

Use an old Slinky as a note- or photo-holder. Flip a Slinky into a half circle so that both ends rest on a flat surface. Lace a twist tie or piece of string through a few coils on each end and tie together. Slide pictures, cards, or notes in between the coils to display.

☀ silver clouds

Keep a few helium-filled Mylar balloons floating around your room. Turn on a fan and bat them around as they float.

☀ comic-book art

Garfield? Peanuts? Frame the covers or pages from a few of your favorite comic books and display them together in a row.

☀ new twist

Tack an old Twister mat onto a wall for a fun plastic polka-dot poster!

☀ house of cards

Cut the backs off old greeting cards. About an inch and a half from each corner, cut half-inch slits into each side. (Shorter sides may only need one slit.) Create a greeting-card house by sliding cards into slits. Display it on a shelf and add a new floor after each holiday or birthday! (Don't want to ruin your greeting cards? Use an old deck of playing cards instead.)

☀ shadow box

Buy a 3-D frame, also known as a shadow box, and display your fave fashion doll, action figure, or stuffed animal inside.

☀ chalk it up

Make a "to-do" chalkboard. Find an old frame you'd like to hang in your room. Measure the size of the frame and paint a rectangular section of a wall with chalkboard paint to match that size. Let dry, then hang the old frame around the painted chalkboard.

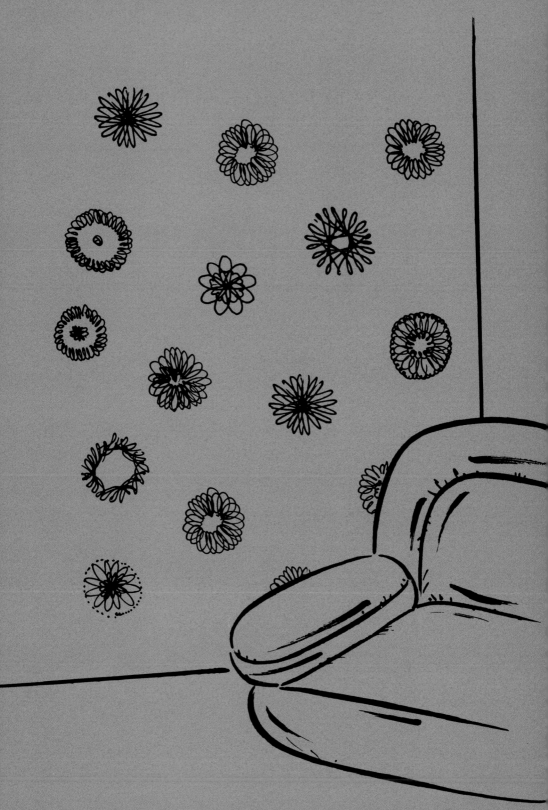

✹ Spirographic

Swirl Spirographs on your wall for a great graphic look (get permission first). Tape or hold the outer gear firmly on the wall to make sure it stays put while you draw your graph with an inner gear. Use different colored pencils to draw with—just be sure to keep the points sharp. Works best on smooth surfaces. If you're not allowed to draw Spirographs directly onto the wall, make them on paper, frame, and hang!

Good Fortune

chinese lanterns
Hang a string across a corner of your room and dangle red paper lanterns from it.

water fountain
Balance all your energy with the calming sound of rushing water. Save up for an electric water fountain, or simply buy a CD with the sounds of a babbling brook.

penny jar
Can the clutter. Use metal or glass kitchen canisters to hold all those lucky pennies you pick up—and other small things you want to keep under control.

lucky bamboo
Hold a stalk of bamboo (available at garden stores) in the middle of a glass and fill it three-quarters of the way with small stones. Add water and watch your fortune grow!

paper dragons

Crisscross two chopsticks and tie them together. Hang origami dragons from the sticks using fishing line of different lengths.

fortune box

Collect fortunes from fortune cookies and put them in a small Chinese take-out box (ask for an extra one next time you order take-out). Keep them by your bed and read a new fortune each morning.

welcome kitty

Put a fortune cat figurine (available at Asian specialty stores) in your room. It may bring you good luck and prosperity. Look familiar? Hello Kitty was modeled after her!

bed rug

Place a bamboo mat beside your bed.

the **Room Doctor** is in!

Got the blues about your room?
Visit the Room Doctor and **find the cure** for what ails you. You'll get **great tips and ideas** on sharing with a sister, getting the privacy you crave, even making cleaning fun!

Always a Mess

My room is always a mess. My mom tells me to clean it up, so I do. But it always gets messy again. How do I keep my room clean?
Always a Mess

If you throw a dirty sock or two on the floor one night, you may think, **"What's the harm?"** But the truth is those two socks on the floor will make it really easy for you to add your muddy jeans to the pile the next day, and your sweaty soccer uniform the next, and so on. After a week, the idea of clearing that **mountain of laundry** becomes a much bigger challenge than just throwing a pair of socks in the hamper.

The real key to keeping your room tidy is to **clean up a little each day.** Spend three minutes at the same time every day—before school, after school, before bed, or whenever—to straighten up. Put those socks you kicked off in the middle of the night into the hamper. (If you don't have one, get one!) Take your empty water glass to the kitchen. Gather up all the hair elastics cluttering up your dresser and put them in a little glass jar. If you **make a habit out of it,** you may soon find yourself doing it automatically every day instead of having to think about it and dread doing it. At the end of the week you'll find **less mess, a happy mom,** and **more time to do what you really want to do.**

But Cleaning Is

Who wouldn't agree? Here's how to **make it fun!**

This Old Room

Pretend you're on a home improvement TV show and explain to the "audience" everything you do. "The real secret to vacuuming is to move things around and vacuum under them, not just around them. This, boys and girls, is an idea you *can* try at home!"

Disco Dust

Turn on some tunes, add some special-effects lighting, and grab a feather duster. Wipe away all the dust as you dance from one corner to another.

Swap Meet

Ask a friend to come over and help you clean—and make sure you return the favor when she's in need. You can help each other discover hidden treasures and decide what to get rid of. Who better to ask "When was the last time you wore that?" or "Why don't you ever wear this?" than a friend?

Play Hoops

Slam-dunk your dirty laundry into the hamper. Go into your closet for a few layups to put away your clean clothes. Make a basket with stuff you don't need—a wastebasket, that is!

Boring!

Before and After

Got a big mess to tackle? Take a photo of your room in all its glorious mess. Then get it as clean as you can and take an "after" picture. You'll be amazed at your handiwork.

Once Upon a Time

You have a masquerade ball to get to by 12 noon, but first you have to clean your room! You'll save time if you dress for the ball before you start. Don your craziest dress-up outfit or costume and start sweeping. If you don't finish by noon, your room will turn into a pumpkin!

Saturday Morning Survivor

When Mom says, "Turn off that TV and go clean your room!" challenge your sibs to see who can finish first. The winner gets immunity the entire day—she gets to choose the games to play and the shows to watch. Warning: if you're caught stuffing things under the bed, you'll be kicked off the island!

Room for Two?

I share a room with my sister. If I re-do my room, I want to decorate it with what I like: sports and the outdoors. But my sister is totally different. She likes, well, girly-girl stuff. Can you help us out?

Room for Two?

Start by finding out what both of you have in common: **Make a list** of the top-five things that you like—colors, teams, stuffed animals, whatever—and have your sister do the same. Then **compare the lists** to see if there are any matches. Maybe you both listed butterflies? That's a theme that would fit your outdoorsy style and her girly style. Did you both list blue as a favorite color? There are many shades—sky blue, turquoise, powder blue. Next time you're at a hardware or discount department store, look at paint chips in the paint section to see if there's a color that suits you both. No matches? List more favorites.

Keep in mind that **you may have to compromise** a little: if your sister agrees to your snowboarding poster, you should agree to her ballerina poster—but try displaying them in similar frames for a more "together" look. The important thing is that both of you wind up with a room that you like spending time in.

Quiz!
Two's Company?

Take this quiz with your roommate to find
a style that you can share!

My 5 Favorite Things	Your 5 Favorite Things
1.	1.
2.	2.
3.	3.
4.	4.
5.	5.

Now compare your lists. Write down your favorites in the circle
on the left. Have your roommate write down her favorites in the
circle on the right. Any matches? Write them in the center.
These things can give you ideas for decorating your room.
No matches? Keep those lists going!

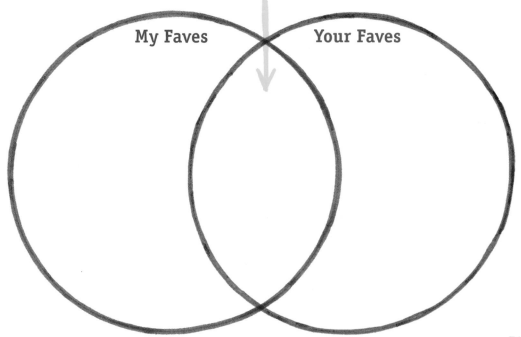

Here's what
we both like!

My Faves   Your Faves

Room for Change

Before Feng Shui

Furniture too close together

Dirty windows

All the furniture pushed against the wall

Lots of square things

Empty vase

Clutter everywhere

Wastebasket in front of doorway

Bare wood floor

We've made a few changes in this room based on *feng shui* (fung SCHWAY), a Chinese way of understanding how the space you live in makes you feel. Take a look at the before and after pictures to see what a difference they make. Then try some feng shui in your own room!

After Feng Shui

Clean windows make for a brighter room!

Leave enough space around furniture so you can move around easily.

Try placing your furniture at an angle for added interest.

Flowers or plants add life to your room.

Too many sharp edges may make you uneasy. Add pillows and plants to make the rough edges softer on the eye.

Clean surfaces make for a clear mind and fewer distractions.

A clear path to the door helps you go with the flow.

Add a rug to wood floors to make your room seem warmer and more comfy.

Desperate

My room is all pink and white stripes. I think it is too girly. Instead I want a blue tie-dye room, but that would mean changing my walls and carpet. I already asked my parents, but they think it'll be too expensive. How can I change their minds?

Desperate for Blue Tie-Dye

You don't have to change everything in your room all at once. Although magazines and catalogues always picture rooms in which *everything* matches, that usually isn't the case with most girls' rooms—or even adults' rooms! Try talking with your parents about letting you introduce **a little bit** of tie-dye into your room at a time. Discuss **ideas that won't cost a lot** of money. "Shop" the house for things that you can try out your new theme on. For example, with old sheets, fabric dye, and a little practice, you can make your own set of tie-dye sheets. Or talk with your parents about the possibility of selling the "girly" things you don't want or need to **raise money** for the new things.

Take it **one idea at a time,** and you may end up with the room of your dreams without emptying your parents' pocketbook.

No Privacy!

I can't get any privacy! I have my own room, but my sister and brother don't understand the word "knock." When I'm gone, my brother goes in and reads my private journal!
No Privacy!

Before you ask your parents to install a lock on your door, think about other ways to **convince your sibs to respect your private space.**

Try talking with them about your room being just that: "yours." When the door is closed, they should knock first before coming in. Explain also that if you don't invite them in, it's because you want time to yourself—and that's really what having your own room is all about. It's a retreat away from things—family, noise, whatever. **It's your place to just be you.**

Follow up your talk by posting **a sign or doorknob hanger** on your door that **reminds them to knock** or to let them know that you'd like to be left alone. Write "Please Knock First!" on one side of the sign, for when their interruptions are O.K., and "Come Back Later" on the other, for when you want to be by yourself.

If all else fails, ask your parents to help you set "knock first" as a house rule and to back you up when the rule is broken. You also may want to **find a secret place** to hide stuff you don't want your sibs to see—and consider getting a journal with a lock!

Girls' Fix-It Guide

Too Messy?

My room used to be really, really messy. Finally one day I told myself to make signs and write things on them like, "You want to wear that sweater tomorrow? Better pick it up off the floor." I posted them around the room, and now I'm over that bad habit.

Marie, **Minnesota**

To clean my room, I went through every single part of it, making three piles—the first pile was to give away, the second was to throw away, the third was to keep. After that, I went out and bought things that were more me.

Sarah, **Missouri**

I used to push things under my bed so that my room looked clean. But I was really making a bigger mess that I would just have to clean up later. So I bought large plastic containers that fit under my bed. That way when I'm in a rush, I can put all my things in the containers. It made my room much cleaner and helped get me organized.

Amy, **Rhode Island**

I had TONS of stuff! So I painted plain boxes to match my wallpaper and comforter. Then I filled the boxes with things that I don't use very often. Not only does it keep my stuff organized, it makes my room look great!

Amy, **Virginia**

Too Crowded?

My room was way too crammed. It seemed like every time I walked into it, I had to look down to see if I was stepping on the ground or something else! So I thought carefully about what I really needed in my room, and I put the rest in storage.

Jenny, Indiana

I had too many things that I didn't really use. So I decided to have a garage sale and sell them. I used the money to buy things I will use!

Lisa Marie, Washington

Too Baby?

I used to have this cartoony comforter. It was a total embarrassment. So I flipped it over, and now I have a white comforter!

Mandy, Wisconsin

My room is pink but I'm not allowed to redecorate it yet. So I added stuff like CD racks, pictures, and a floor lamp to make it look more grown-up.

Deb, Pennsylvania

77

Too Blah?

Try rearranging the furniture. One day I got bored and decided to move everything around. It'll feel like you are walking into a new room!

Andrea, **United Kingdom**

Can you say booor-ing? My walls used to be all white. So I painted one wall orange, one yellow, one lime green, and one blue. Now I love spending time in my room!

Leah, **Virginia**

My room was really plain and messy. To fix it, I put in shelves and hung up a bunch of stuff that shows "me" — my jerseys, posters, and pictures.

Melissa, **Alaska**

When I got bored with my bedspread, I went out and bought two solid-colored sheet sets and mixed and matched them so they look cool. Once I showed my Mom how responsible and serious I was about changing my room, she chipped in and bought me a nice quilt.

Nattalia, **New York**

To change your room, you need to look at it and think, "What interests me?" I like dance, so I added some dance figurines and posters. Make your room a place that you can be yourself and be creative!

Vanessa, **Canada**

My room was too big and plain, so I filled it with my personality. I blew up pictures of my friends and hung them on the walls. I got more colorful things and put posters of things I was interested in on the walls. I had a great time filling my room up with me!

Sephia, Washington

If you're in the ARGH! mood with your room, decorate it with the things you love. Think of it as your place.

Emily, Indiana

My parents wouldn't let me repaint or get new curtains and bedding and all that. Instead I made a huge poster collage to take away the boringness of it all. It made my room look really cool and centered the attention on my beautiful collage.

Abby, New York

Too Small?

If you hang mirrors in your room, they will reflect the light and walls and make your room seem bigger.

Angela, Alaska

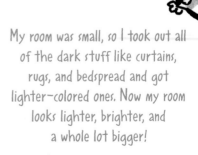

I did not have much room to play because my bed was right in the middle of the room. So I moved it up against the wall. Now I have plenty of room.

Emily, Texas

My room was small, so I took out all of the dark stuff like curtains, rugs, and bedspread and got lighter-colored ones. Now my room looks lighter, brighter, and a whole lot bigger!

Alicia, Massachusetts